RIFT

Also by Forrest Hamer

*Call & Response* (1995)
*Middle Ear* (2000)

# RIFT

## POEMS BY FORREST HAMER

Four Way Books
New York City

Distributed by
University Press of New England
Hanover and London

Editorial Office
Four Way Books
POB 535, Village Station
New York, NY 10014
www.fourwaybooks.com

Library of Congress Catalogue Card Number: 2006928237

ISBN: 978-1-884800-75-7

Cover photograph: *Rift* by Jeff T. Alu. By permission of the artist.

Cover design: K. C. Witherell/Hello Studio.

This book is manufactured in the United States of America and printed on acid-free paper.

Four Way Books is a not-for-profit literary press. We are grateful for the assistance we receive from individual donors, public arts agencies, and private foundations.

This publication is made possible with public funds from the National Endowment for the Arts and from the New York State Council on the Arts, a state agency.

Distributed by University Press of New England
One Court Street, Lebanon, NH 03766

[clmp]

We are a proud member of the Council of Literary Magazines and Presses.

## Acknowledgments

*American Poetry Review:*
 "Account"
 "Initiation"
 "What Happened"
*Antioch Review:*
 "Selfless"
*Callaloo:*
 "Assisted Living (Goldsboro Narrative #44)"
 "Letter from Cuba"
 "Mercy"
 "Reconciliation"
 "Some Sugar"
 "Someone I Know" (*As he was walking by our porch...*)
 "Suicide Prevention (Goldsboro Narrative #43)"
*Electronic Poetry Review:*
 "Someone I Know" (*When, during the first act...*)
 "Someone I Know" (*Some of us have to live with being mean*)
 "Someone I Know" (*...thinks I failed at writing him down*)
*Five Fingers Review:*
 "A Body of Thought"
 "Someone I Know" (*For almost two years after he died...*)
*Luna:*
 "Someone I Know" (*In the middle of a memory...*)
 "Someone I Know" (*A woman late in her 80s began once more to feel...*)
*nocturnes (re)view:*
 "Lost"
 "The Conquest"
 "What I Wish I Could Tell You"
*Ploughshares:*
 "Goldsboro Narrative #27"
 "Goldsboro Narrative #45"
*SHADE 2004:*
 "Discourse"
 "My Personal Epistemology"
 "Poem"
 "The Point of the Story"
*Shenandoah:*
 "Ninety-Five, a Hundred"
*ZYZZYVA:*
 "Common Betrayal"

Many thanks to the California Arts Council for an artist's fellowship; to
Martha Rhodes at Four Way Books; to the editors of the journals in which
many of these poems first appeared; to the Squaw Valley Community of
Writers for their reliable support; to the students and fellow faculty of the
Callaloo Creative Writing Workshops; and to Dan Bellm, Lucille Clifton,
Molly Fisk, Diana Garcia, Jeanne Harasemovitch, Richard Harris,
Alice Jones, Susan Kolodny, Lynne Knight, Afaf Mahfouz, Purnima Mehta,
Harryette Mullen, G.E. Patterson, Charles Henry Rowell,
Murray Silverstein, KwanLam Wong, John Yau and Yu-Wen Ying,
among very many, for the conversations.

# Table of Contents

**Someone I Know**

**The Point of the Story**

Speak speak so we may know the end of this travel.
—Mahmoud Darwish

## Reconciliation

I don't know what kind of man I am.

I know it was not hate I felt;
It was not the disgust and the stone in my belly.

The world is a mystery and they were my question.


We were strangers again.

# My Brother, My Sister

## Aftermath

A      Somewhere there are omens.
B      Somewhere all the bodies have been buried, and survivors keep watch
C   *pre*  Over skeletons they also had been.
D      The children are raising each other.

A &-B  Bodies are buried; survivors keep watch.
     B  Somewhere the earth is burning, eager for new skin.
C &- D  Each child is raising another;
    D  Music and meaning are patient.

A &-B  The earth is just burning.
     B  There are terrible questions—
C &- D  Somewhere music is patient, and meaning.
    D  Somewhere those who had been slaughtered feel unanswerable longing.

We have terrible questions,
And those who slaughtered have longing.
Those who have been slaughtered lie unanswered.
Languages lift from ashes like these

And those who slaughtered feel the same longing.
Hope comes home, somewhere in us;
Language lifts from ash.
Rightly, we are cautious.

Somewhere hope hovers over  *over (prep) same line*
What we would have done, whatever did we do.
Rightly, we are cautious;
Stories everywhere.

7

For almost two years after he died, I could still feel him touching me. Lying down or sitting, I sensed his press on my skin; or, walking, I'd walk up almost into him. I have other memories of him, but they are only ideas.

In my baby book are pictures of a woman who cared for me during the three years we lived in Germany. She spoke very little English, I'm told, and my dead mother tells me I was bereft when finally we had to leave her. I wonder where she is in me, why German sounds so strange.

Increasingly, strangers look like people I'm sure I've known. Some are the children of schoolmates, and they look the way I remember their parents. Some have moved here from North Carolina or Texas or Connecticut; others I just haven't seen in California for years. **Someone I know** is certain we met in another lifetime, a whole continent away, and she is convinced this is not the last time we'll have to say goodbye to each other.

O poem, hopeful body.

Body of the poem

# My Personal Epistemology

I don't know what to believe, sometimes.

There are a few people I have known
With whom we knew what the other was thinking,
And sometimes we were thinking of each other
For exactly the same reason.  We knew not to dismiss this as only chance.
I would know something was very wrong with my friend, for instance,
And when I called him the first thing he would say was,
I knew it would be you.

I believe the proof of an idea about the world lies
In the world of the personal, and the personal is evidence of being meaning-
Fully in the world.
I believe the truth of language lies in who is speaking.
I don't know if knowledge and belief are speaking the same thing.

I often believed that, wherever in the world
I was, I would know the exact moment each of my parents died,
But I don't know why
That didn't really happen with my mother
And what that will mean about my father.

Because I was not saved, my family began to worry
About my eternal soul.  I told them I didn't believe as they did,
And what seemed to hurt us most
In all this was what we all now knew.

When, during the first act, **someone I know** walked on stage, her mother and her father and her sisters and her brother and some of her cousins began to clap, and one among them said, there's Daughter, and the daughter paused, smiled a slight smile, and went back to her character. The mystery captivated everyone, even those who knew none of the teenagers on stage.

Each Easter, each Christmas, and sometimes during the summer, Daughter helps the children in her church put on a pageant. The older ones come because they have to, and none of them likes the practice it takes to become somebody else.

The mystery was the murderer, Daughter the character wanting earnestly to help detectives solve the crime no one could believe had happened, her heroine careful and poised in the face of various suspicions.

Once, all three wise men looked out from the pulpit stage and became terrified, and not one of them heeded the girl standing to the side, speaking all of their parts.

## Ninety-Five, a Hundred

Let's say the self is a story.

Just ask my siblings, they'll tell you:
In the family we grew up in,
Only adults could tell lies
Or call someone a liar;
Children had to call lies stories.
For a little while, my sister and I helped
Tell my brother the story of Santa Claus;
It seemed like a nice thing to do.
But Santa Claus terrified my brother:
One night, when the family was driving
Down Center Street, Santa Claus waving
From the Western Auto window,
My brother leapt across the front seat,
Afraid of being seen.
Our story was never fun for him,
Even when he got the toys he wanted.

So, call the self a story. My siblings refuse
To tell their children lies about Santa Claus.
They want them to know
Where the Christmas gifts come from;
They want them only accountable to God.
Their brother is another story.

The three of us used to play
Hide-and-go-seek for what seemed like forever.
One of us would count time down in a song
While the other two went looking
In all the spaces of our house
For somebody's next surprise.

## Someone I Know

As he was walking by our porch, one of my aunts whispered to her sister that the man I'd never seen before had died and been brought back to life. The other aunt frowned, sucked her teeth, and warned her sister about saying such things so loud the children could hear. I couldn't be sure what I'd heard, and, since I knew not to ask, I waited for the next time the man passed by our porch.

Everybody must have some kind of father somewhere, the gang of us figured. And we walked my cousin's father into imagination so we could ask him what it was like to go away so far.

All day one day, my cousin and I had been riding our bikes, and a church we could swear was never there appeared, and inside the cool place a man waited alone and dressed in his casket. We sat on the first pew, dangling our legs. We looked close at the man, but didn't know him.

When those who had known Lazarus saw him again, after the long days of their doubt, they couldn't help but feel he was not the one he had been.

# Initiation

After I stumbled through the gauntlet, after they had hit me
(As hard as they could,)
Some there only because there was somebody else
To be brought in, I joined them
In greeting the new ones, the frightened and longing ones,
And I punched as hard and as much as I could, something
Filling in me I would tell you was a thrill
Only because I had no better word for it./
There was another word for it: violence
Made my mother impatient with me, she would call me evil,
And I knew what she was trying to talk to me about—
How much I hated,
How much I wanted and how greedy wanting made me.
What I wanted most were better words.

*Why one stanza?.*

13

*In 1994, some 800,000 Rwandan Tutsis were killed
during a three-month campaign led by Rwandan Hutus;
the first targets, though, were Hutu moderates.*

A  We listened to what they had to say, and felt ourselves
B  Becoming cold, inflamed
C  With their betrayal, the lies they told themselves;
D  Our brothers were as dangerous as

A← B  We were becoming cold. Inflamed,
B  We hated, we couldn't wait to kill.
C← D  Our brothers were as dangerous as
D  Those fools! Placing themselves between

A← B  The ones we couldn't wait to kill,
B  Our furies; confusing us with cautions.
C ←D  Such fools! Placing themselves in the middle!
D  How could they be right if we were right?

A ←B  Their caution was confusing—   *confusion create break or confusion in pattern*
B  How could we be right if they were right?
C ← D  How could we not be right?
D  We had machetes, hoes, a hallowed will.

A← B  How could we be right and they be right?
B  We found them in each other's pleading arms;
C ←D  We had machetes, hoes, a hallowed will;
D  We stunned them in their beds and on the street.

A← B  We found them in each other's pleading arms.
B  We mowed them down more quickly than we vowed.
C ←D  We left them in their beds and on the streets.
D  Blessed by our success, we hunted Tutsis.

14

A  B   We mowed them down more quickly than we vowed—
   B   Tutsis, now less distinct than ever.
C  D   Blessed by this success,
   D   We would never have to deal with them again.

A  B   Tutsis, now less distinct than ever
   B   From those lies they told themselves—
C  D   We would never have to deal with them again.
   D   They should have listened.

15

## hat I Wish I Could Tell You

I wish I could tell you something
about that state of mind
something about that body I was in
the thoughts sensations perceptions
within that state of mind
[I was making the moment]
the thoughts sensations perceptions
history already
I was making the moment that moment *state of mind*
[I was forgetting]
and the people the history already
[as they were the way they looked]
I was forgetting and the people
their eyes held me
[as they were then the way they looked]
regarding the future they were
how their eyes held me
wishing they were telling me
the future they were wishing the past *history*
they were going
to what they were telling me
something about that body I was in (1)
the past I was going to be (2)
something I wish I could tell you.

16

*why one paragraph?*

*★ time ★
★ pattern ★
★ word play
layering
texturizing*

# Discourse

And I said to him, we are continuous,
And whatever the self is, it is never
As we would consider, so I don't believe the possibility
Of speaking too much of it; and he says to me,
Continuous, exactly, with what?

What about the body: something is always pulling at it
—gravity, responsibility, the life after this one.

My siblings and I don't speak to each other
As much as we used to.  When one of us calls, we talk
About the care of our father, our aunts, and then
We talk about the children.  In the pauses, we acknowledge
How different from each other we've become,
And each of us somehow considers how much
We miss the way things briefly were.

## Across the Gulf

*Suppose there is nothing one finally keeps from another;*
He who used to be my father
Wandered into someone else's room, and my sister took his arm,
Whispering I was waiting for him outside,
And for a moment he remembered; he brightened;

*That of all we never say or think or know,*
*It is the same for all of us.*
*And in each brain, what matters drifts apart*
*And is unreconciled,*
Then the water took him back under—

He looked at me without knowing me
*The self not really private and distinct, just brief.*
And bristled when I reached
Just to touch him.

## Poem

Sometimes, after, its small fire still

thrumming just under my skin, I
am in awe of this self, sensing once more

I am not what I would think, not body (*early winter light holding against late day chill*);

not the end of this one conception;

but the nature of awe
and the nature of doubting it.

# What Happened

To say about it one thing. No, two. It was a horror. It could not be spoken.
So first there was the problem of recovering speech.
Calling out to it, listening each other.
We looked to the assurances of nature—regular violence, regular relief.
Color splayed before us—yellows, rhythms of red.
Faces and patterns in faces. Patience. W .C.
Finally, a word, but not many.
Silence again, longing.
More words but not what happened; words we had already said.
Horror holding, a black hole. Opening a little,
Then a little more, then: we could think about the horror: what happened
A kind of speech, but not yet.

*resolution,*
*why not on*
*another line?*

20

# Goldsboro Narrative #27

2 The dark and heavy coat she always wore hid
  From her as much as anyone

1 What grew her belly out one thought at a time.

2 And she who did not know her body,
  Who was surprised to feel it

1 Created with some boy she'd barely met,

2 Ignored the word so much a shock
  She was someone who used to be herself.

1 She was as stunned as anyone to learn

2 A newborn was found inside
  A trash bin, the trail winding its way back to someone

1 We all thought we knew.

# The Continents Still Ache for Each Other

## Common Betrayal

In another poem, I was afraid *)enjambent*
Of becoming a woman.

I know now we are always becoming something else.

How brief is a seeming thing! Quickly *nice*
We are gone, *(quick line)* *enjambent*

Making poems that stay behind
Waving at us *(quick line behind)*

And waving us on.

## A Body of Thought

Think of any two people you imagine making
  love to each other, and what this loving has to do
  with you
Think about the relation between this
  and that: one thought and what would be a thought
Think of all those ways It makes one humble
  The two of them fumbling with clothes and then
  with such frank beauty.  O,

Think of thought breaking
  into vast lands longing
  And think of this creation and all the ways there
  are The two of us impelled
  towards a moment
  oblivious, always, to that which thinks us up.

## Diaspora

*[handwritten: Nice stanza form]*

*[handwritten: nice line-break]*

Fires whirr in dervishes below us, magnets
    Churn the oceans, and the earth spins
Imperceptibly fast; blood rushes through us
    On its way to who knows where; and the heart
Is moved by the something that set in

*[handwritten: momentum]*

    Motion does not stop until another contravenes.
Otherwise we would go on
    Forever, moving and being moved,
Which is how we speak of the soul,
    Which is a current that would not be stopped.

*[handwritten: cross stanza]*

We cross vast landscapes and are moved
    By vastness: it intrigues us, sets us in perpetual longing.
Some people are vast forces in themselves:
    I know someone who seeks
To teach and love and to serve.


    I know someone else who is unhappy,
Who is a force not of evil but
    Dispersal: this despair destroys things.
I am moved by them both;
    I am moved by these problems

Of my heart. Peoples move each other
    Over expanses of land and belief.
The currents we are manifest as
    What it is we feel, the world
We are making being made still.

*[handwritten annotations: "visual form lets us see spinning earth within spinning poem)"; "but stop on line break + stanza break"; "line break creates a look of word definition or explanation"; "enjambed stanza"; "good w.c. to end on"]*

27

## Goldsboro Narrative #45

The whites and the blacks are still newcomers.
You can tell: the way we claim flags, that we fight.
The other nomads were moved on, learning that land
does not love humans and is not at home with us,
even when it lets us grow ourselves food,
even when it lets us house our dead.
In some hundreds of years, this land will shrug us off
its wet and itching skin, tell us once more,
*Get on.*

# Some Sugar

*You ain't mad, is you? Then give me some sugar.* [layering]
My aunt wants a kiss from us, wants us to forgive her
want for the sugar her body doesn't take.

Near eighty, she has become a patient nurses do not like.
At times we do not like her either, and often are mad with her
for sneaking candy into the house,

shocked at how bald the curses are. [She doesn't like her life [layer]
without sugar] doesn't want to be old without
what she has loved for so long,

walking herself three times a day to buy sweets
and a Goody's powder.  Now, one of her toes has been taken,
others may go.  She doesn't walk but still she wants

her sweets, bribes some cousins to sneak
cookies past her sisters who worry they cannot care
well enough for her at home.

My aunt asks if we are mad and doesn't wait
to be answered, knows we will bend to
kiss her, laugh at how impossible she's become,

how funny she can be.  The truth be told it's hard
enough living our own lives out, going along with what is best or right
but doesn't always seem so. [tension]

[texture] Hungers having not much to do with us make us
hold on to each other,
forgive each other what we finally do.

time — in what went on
before the additional comment

Dialogue
5 stanza
5 lines/stanza

## Severance

( ) And she said to me, It is the self
which alienates us
from our purposes.
We were talking about suffering
*When I had walked far away*

*from my life,*
and its lessons, and she said she had not been able to learn
from all of her work,
works I would say were good ones
*and I lay one night in a forest cleared*

*once a human lifetime by fires,*
but she admitted
~~selfishness had moved her more~~
than doing good.
*I learned of my briefness,*

*the very urgency of my purposes;*
Well, I said, So what?
Maybe the self is also
one of our purposes—
*and the next day I grew ready to get back*

*the life I'd been having,*
how separateness leaves us
this illusion of having become
so alien, we cannot help *this time to join it*
but let the self go.

30

# Mercy

And my father took me to some woods *precarious warning*
Outside the town I thought was already too familiar,
Already too small, and he brought along a shotgun
He would be leaving behind—a 12-gauge,
Comfortable against the length of my arm,
Straight as an eye eager for its aim.
*Keep it firm against your shoulder,* he warned,
*And watch out for its kick.* And I who thought already
I was careful enough, and knew more than everything,
Sighted myself at the tin can he set on a tree stump.
I pulled the trigger, noticing its give—not too light,
But not heavy—and the shotgun lurched
Back against my right shoulder, nearly knocking me down;
And I gave the gun back, swallowing what I knew

*↑Stanza break*

Could be a sob, betrayed by the shotgun and my body.
It was almost the last time I have fired a gun.
It stayed unloaded in my father's closet while he was away,
And after he returned from Vietnam, and had retired,
My mother had him keep it on the back porch behind the freezer.
We forgot it was there. But a few years ago, after my mother died,
It became clear how far my father's mind had gone.
We had to take away his car keys; keep him from getting lost.
We also had to think how he could hurt himself
Without knowing, or someone else during furious fits.
I found the gun and loaded it again against my shoulder,
Still impressed. The trigger itched to be kicked, making me see
The misery my father wandered through was just no way
To live, and not the way I would have him die.

31

**Someone I Know**

## Lost

Like the one who went wandering off
looking
and hasn't since been seen


Like our sense of his woods


Like that dry day in the desert when we climbed
into the living
spring mountains
and it began snowing and hailing
and we were happy by it


Like the conversation we are
about the wondering
and sight


Like this sense of where he might be still


Like the idea there
is no idea
no before and no later
no death
and not now


Like the drive back down
and the heavy heat
insisting
You were not just there

# Letter from Cuba

It takes two full days away before I stop worrying about my work.
On the third day, I go back to stops on the tour from the day before; and by
    the end of the fourth day, whether I see more sights no longer matters.
After a week, I think I could leave my life.

I have been here longer than I can say.
There are moments I am in Goldsboro or Mobile or Savannah, and it is the
    time we are children and the weather hot, and the people mostly our
    family, and the air is fragrant with flowers, mud stink, and kerosene,
    and there are crops to be cut.

My heart is nearly breaking.
One afternoon, I sat in the white sand and looked across the Atlantic.
I thought how long ago some of us ended up here and some of us ended up
    there.
Restlessness still washes me over in waves.

Kind and handsome men come up to me to practice their English, they
    want to sell me cigars and rum, a cheaper room, a meal at a cousin's
    paladar, a woman, themselves.
No, no, I say. I want you to tell me the stories.
We walk or we sit down and eat, and I listen, asking, I'd like please to
    practice my Spanish.
When you see me again, my brother, my sister, I will be calmer.

The Yoruba priest tossed cowrie shells several times at my feet, telling me to
    make offerings to hold on to my money, to be protected from accidents,
    for me to be married.
He told me I could change, if I wanted.
He didn't know what I wanted him to know about me.
And I was surprised to learn what I wanted.

One day, walking the center of Havana, I tripped and fell to my knees.
I'd been looking up at crumbling buildings, I was listening to music
    coming from someone's open windows, and I was trying to place a
    voice.
Everyone moved toward me with concern.
I'm fine, I kept saying in English, thank you.
It's true what they say: there is beautiful music here, and it is everywhere.

There is music some places in the world that makes me wish.
Instead of settling down, I could have wandered.
I could have loved some others; I could have loved much more.
I could have lived other lives.

*Where you from, Martinique? Bahamas? Americano? You like Tupac?*
I'm not sure I know the America they ask me about.
I tell them I listen to the blues. I tell them I listen to opera.
Sometimes, on the way home from work, I hear salsa.

The poet who read only in Spanish made me close my eyes.
I was falling and falling into a voice.
Not knowing her language, I finally heard the poems.
And when it was my turn, mi hermana, mi hermano, waters swelled deep
    within me, and I spoke back.

*chilling*  ·  *5 stanzas*

## Suicide Prevention (Goldsboro Narrative #43)

I was calling because I wanted
to say it out loud
to someone
who had heard someone else say,
I want to kill my *own* self.

→ *is it really funny?!?!*

And I had thought of myself as *funny*
and I knew it was more
than a phase,
and I was damned,
but I wanted to say that out loud, too,

to someone who had heard
unspeakable things
spoken
by those they would never suppose
lived screaming beneath

*↑ break, tension*

whispering voices.
And I was calling
to learn
what living might be like
after I had finished

this frightening phone call,
still wanting perhaps to die but
no longer
wanting really to kill
myself.

            *for C. and for B.*

38

A woman late in her eighties began once more to feel desire. She said a fever came over her so strong at night she would not sleep: she would imagine all sorts of men, and some women, and all of them left her the sense she probably was dying, the flushes one last rally to keep her self intact.

Some people can feel full only when passion is strong, so they provoke others into making them feel. Others can feel only themselves when feeling is calmed or seems gone. And there are others whose sense of being comes from not being selves at all. **Someone I know** doesn't yet know what there is to tell, and I spend hours with him waiting for the song there is when I hear best: sung by me in a language I do not recognize, listening fills me with the closest I have come to being satisfied.

*I would not be beautiful, for that would be another curse; nor would I be on fire. The first curse, of course, is knowing.*

# Assisted Living (Goldsboro Narrative #44)

1.

Down the hall from Mr. Frank's room is where Miss Naomi stays.

She wheels herself up and down the hall before lunch, but after the
    afternoon snack of Cheetos and Lorna Doones, she knocks on Mr.
    Frank's door and asks him to be her escort.

This upsets the day attendant, Marlene, who thinks Miss Naomi has been
    too used all her life to men's attentions.

Marlene thinks Mr. Frank is just too nice.

Mr. Frank doesn't seem to mind, but when his son comes over and watches
    TV shows from the 60s, or when Mr. Frank's daughter comes to visit
    with her two quiet boys or Mr. Frank's two sisters-in-law, Mr. Frank
    complains about having to keep his apartment door closed, and having to
    pretend once in a while he can't hear someone knocking.

Aside from this, Mr. Frank likes the new place.

He sometimes doesn't know where he is, but he knows this is where he
    belongs.

Two years ago, this was flat, pine-lined land, just past the ends of the city
    Mr. Frank moved to once he got married.

His wife's people had died one by one in this town, and one day so did his
    wife, but there were still a few family left and two of them were his
    children.

Sometimes he didn't recognize exactly who they were—he'd call his boy his
    brother, speak to his daughter like she was his mother, and it was good
    for once to have all his kinfolk in the same town.

Mr. Frank gets ashamed sometimes by Miss Naomi's interest in him.
He's too old, he tells his son, to have anything to do with _that mess_.
Marlene thinks Mr. Frank should just relax and finally let himself be taken
    care of.
Miss Naomi thinks Marlene should mind her own business, and let Mr.
    Frank get used to being here.

2.

Because they still expect to be protected,
the brothers are quiet and polite in adult company.
When they are at home in their room,
the younger one talks and talks, even in his sleep,
and his brother draws powerful saviors who arrive
just when they are needed.

The two boys are close together in age,
but Jamal remembers his grandmother telling her sisters
the brothers couldn't be more different.
And she said they were as close to each other
as she and her sisters were, she the talkative one,
one or the other of her sisters serious or funny.

But none of the sisters could draw, so Jamal wonders
where this comes from in him,
neither his mother nor his father talented this way,
neither of them anxious
by something in the world to be seen.
Jamal wants to make a picture for his grandfather.

At first he thought to draw another savior,
but in the last few days he has begun to sense
something forming in him as a mood.
He recognizes this in his grandfather
who sometimes stays more quiet than he can be, who stares
at people as if he doesn't know them.

42

And because his grandfather's mood consumes every room,
Jamal has wished his mother would forego
taking him and his brother to visit that place.
The feeling appears this time to help him, though,
and Jamal begins believing he might finally be able to make
his grandfather remember him for good.

2 sent
6 lines

Childhood desire
to achieve the
impossible

3.

Maybe living here is a mistake, Maria often thinks.
Maybe this is not the place she thought.
Maybe she should have stayed
where she already comes from, in Manzanillo,
with her sisters and her mother, and the man
she would have married had he asked her

                    not to go.

Maybe Marlene, her friend from church
who has never been from any other place,
is wrong, and Maria will never belong,
even if they bury her in the limed ground

                  right under.

Maybe the children she teaches
are not her children, in the end, not the ones who speak
her languages, whose moods she keeps

                attuning with her own.

Maybe the restlessness she suffers is as home
as any place, and she has yet to go where she won't flee,
living her memory and the history of her hearts,

                    what her heart might be.

## Selfless

When he found himself falling, and he was falling
into love (*so, THIS is that feeling of being,*
he said to no one in particular),
he opened his eyes and saw him who was looking
back, and each one witnessed
the other less a self than before and
more, and more, but more.

I say to you, the self is promiscuous—most anybody will do;
any body, too; world and worlds—

Know this: falling-apart, fragments-assembling one:
no one in particular is fallen for you, too.

45

In the middle of a memory, someone I can't see becomes **someone I know**. It is the one who, another day in his life, put another needle into his arm and left it there, drawn by sheer whiteness and faint light, walking through the liquid one world from this one.

There are monkeys all over the body of my house, tracking the floor and pulling books from the shelves. Two of them are fucking in a corner, and another one is excited just to see. I say to them, who do you think you are, and they say back to me, don't you remember?

Sometimes you find yourself by looking away. Sometimes, looking is addictive. The one who went looking for light loved to be looked at. He was never really in love with himself, but he didn't want to be forgotten.

**Someone I know** thinks I failed at writing him down.  He thinks I should be ashamed of myself, and when he gets ugly with it, calling me out of my name, people become excited.  What was wrong with me, one man asked him, why did I write so wrong, and the one who was not written says, this man knows nothing about you and me.

Because, perhaps, his memory began to fail him, my father began telling us his stories.  When we heard the betrayal, we understood he'd been too hurt before to speak.  Then, when he accused us of stealing from him, we began to assume he was grieving all of his new losses.  Now, betrayals later, we don't know what to think.

I bet by now you're wanting a story.  I could speak of some feeling and you could recognize one of your own, in your body, and we could let this settle our griefs.  And if the story is this fragment, and this would be the story I could stick with, you wouldn't begrudge me much, would you.

*Excellent*

# The Point of the Story

Some of us have to live with being mean.  One means well, but ends up hurting some other who has no real interest in imagination.  **Someone I know** is confused by everyday niceness, it makes no sense to him, and this perplexes us more than the sense he is shouldering horrors many would say are not his.


In a flicker of a lash, somebody becomes greedy with murder and he can't not think of it even when he considers calm, even when he wants only to drown in some body's water.  He walks until he finds strange streets, dares himself to stop every few feet, see if the panic has let up. He doesn't think he is possessed the way his cousin believes, and he doesn't believe much else.

*6 syll.*

*6 syllab.*

*7 syll.*

This is never easy to say.  *They were so different*, the other ones, we didn't know what to make of it.  But when the ground within us started to give, we held on to each other the best way we could, surprising ourselves with that love.

## The Conquest

Walking right up to the limits of the land, up
Against the brink of our nature,

Bruised bodies refused us the next steps.

We sat, and washed and oiled and blessed each other's feet;
We knelt before the ones we didn't know, them we had hated,
And peeled their heavy boots, and placed their feet
First against the ground
Of our chest then deep into the somber sky beneath.

We walked back to where we were lost,

humbled By all there was we had not seen
By all there was we had.

## Talking Cure

*A man who had been harmed had only one story*
*of it; it was the story he lived*
Let it go, I wish myself
*I wanted to help; I asked him about older stories,*
*I showed him this was bodied*

It stays because it presses to be solved,
and there the problem is
*between us,*
not in the world as in the world within
*I told him some stories of my own*

It was some time ago; it's colored all that's happened
since: this stubborn, nervous way of keeping things
*One day another story moved him;*
*he let it live and let it save his life*
It wants to go.  So, let it

# Account

What I can tell you is that he is my neighbor.
I can tell you we live next to each other in separated worlds.

He stays inside behind shut blinds.
His yard is a mess. He puts out his garbage at night.

His wife keeps to herself, and she looks up only at distance.
Their child plays in the street near the other children, but
none of the children play games together.

Sometimes, my cousin refuses to visit, or when he comes he refuses to stay,
because he remembers the beatings and the prods to his balls.

My brother is convinced my neighbor is responsible this happened.
My sister shakes even at the thought this thing has happened.

My neighbor is losing weight; he is already a small man.
His house needs painting, and the leaves from my tree are choking his drains.

I am thinking of getting two dogs, and I wonder what my neighbor will think.
I am thinking of replacing the fence.
I am thinking of raising my attic, bring light in from the sky.
What will my neighbor think?

What will happen if there is an earthquake, shaking us out of our houses
into the street? Will it be necessary to speak to my neighbor?

Will I ask him about my cousin?
Will I mention the leaves from my tree?
Will I ask him how he raises his child,

whether he and his family need candles?

54

## Table

After, we came back to the house.    Siblings
The three of us sat at the table,
Looking in each other for our parents.
And, as we had already known, together.
We would never make either of them
Whole; and the parts of them we'd give
To lovers and to children    prep phrase
Would never stay them here forever.

*sounds like second poem*

The brother who had not lived
Came from outside to sit with us;
One by one, the best we could,
We were gracious with him.

## The Point of the Story

That next morning, a little depressed, I said, Self,
Don't you finally get tired of yourself?
And the answer was obvious, but not absolute,
Which is, of course, just like a self.
So I countered, What's your point?, uncovering

The whole other realm of questions and conjectures,
Only a few of which make sense.
Over dinner, my friend who was writing another novel
Had said she thought the narrative impulse was too much
With us in the end, even when

We move toward fracture, write towards nonsense.
I agreed with her, lamenting that I sometimes feel
I only tell one story,
And there is always that other side.
As for all of the other stories, Well, you can imagine.

A book has its cover, its author
Probably not a good judge. Despite my best efforts,
I keep coming back to talking to myself.
It's harder and harder to finally tell
Just what I'm saying back.

56

*[handwritten top right: 9 stanzas]*

# Conference

*Durban, 2001*

*[handwritten left margin: A B C D with bracket]*

On South African TV, the nightly news is broadcast four times—
Once each in Zulu, English, Afrikaans, and Xhosa.
Watching them in sequence offers the sense young countries are forged
On very old land, peoples fighting to make of the news what might last.

*[handwritten left margin: A ← B]*
Once each in Zulu, English, Afrikaans, and Xhosa,
B    Someone said, *The self can be a dangerous thing*—
*[handwritten: C ← D]* People fight to make of themselves what might last.
D    There is always an other, and we don't always know what to make of it.

*[handwritten right: Dialogue]*

*[handwritten left margin: R ← B]* Someone else said, *The self may be dangerous,*
B    But if the self is also an us and one becomes lost to it,
*[handwritten: C ← D]* There are always others. What do we make of them *[handwritten: Statement becomes question]*
D    How do they settle our grief?

*[handwritten right: another Dialogue]*

*[handwritten: Statement becomes absolute]*
*[handwritten left margin: A ← B]* The self is an us and the self can get lost.
B    Our table was too small. Some of us sat at the sides of the wall
*[handwritten: C ← D]* Seeking to settle old griefs. *[handwritten: Question becomes action → dialogue becomes voice]*
D    Hearing some things but not others, people demanded to speak.

*[handwritten left margin: A ← B]* *[handwritten: fault to detail]* The roundtable was small. Some sat at the sides of the wall. *[handwritten: remove prep phrase]*
B    There were wounds they were wearing, marks of the many not there.
*[handwritten: C ← D]* Everyone needed to speak and be heard, but *[handwritten: condensed sent + thought → more direct → more feeling]*
D    Horrors had happened; there wasn't room for them all. *[handwritten: little the lack of room at the table → layering]*

*[handwritten: build up]*
*[handwritten left margin: A ← B]* There were wounds upon wounds, marks of the many not there.
B    We were expecting many, not the many who came;
*[handwritten: C ← D]* Horrors had happened and no one had room for them all. *[handwritten: rewording → others don't have room for them, more personal → more discriminating]*
D    A stranger stood, cautioning, *We should not presume.*

*[handwritten: dialogue → forewarning]*

57

A ⌐B He'd been waiting for many, the many who came;

B He wanted to body them in.

C ⌐D And though he'd come far, he couldn't hold hopes;

D Their gravity held him back.


A ⌐B We have to work at it, work for it, body it in.

B Are you talking about peace, I ask him, and he says back to us,

C Even a stone is in movement. I stopped for a moment, taking it in.

D We have to keep going.


A ⌐B But, do we move towards peace, I ask him, and he says to me,

B A self becomes formed by the other it hates;

C We have to question our nature;

D There's some other story to tell.

58

# Notes

Epigraph. This line from Darwish ends the poem "We travel like other people" translated by Abdullah al-Udhari and reprinted in *Against Forgetting: 20th Century Poetry of Witness,* (Norton, 1993), Carolyn Forché, editor.

Page 3, "Reconciliation." This poem emerged out of a review of transcripts of testimony presented before the South African Truth and Reconciliation Commission, and accounts of public testimony presented before the International Criminal Tribunal for Rwanda.

Page 10, "Someone I Know." The poem's ending borrows from Lucille Clifton's "Lazarus," which appears in *Blessing the Boats: New and Selected Poems,* (BOA Editions, 2000).

Page 25, "Common Betrayal." The poem's title borrows from Lynne Knight's *The Book of Common Betrayals,* (Bear Star Press, 2002).

Forrest Hamer is the author of *Call & Response* (Alice James, 1995), which received the Beatrice Hawley Award, and *Middle Ear* (Roundhouse, 2000), which received the Northern California Book Award. He is an Oakland, California, psychologist and affiliate member of the San Francisco Psychoanalytic Institute and Society. His poetry has appeared in many journals, and has been anthologized in *Poet's Choice: Poems for Everyday Life, The Geography of Home: California's Poetry of Place, Making Callaloo: 25 Years of Black Literature, Blues Poems,* and the 1994 and 2000 editions of *The Best American Poetry.* He has received fellowships from the Bread Loaf Writers' Conference and the California Arts Council, and he has taught on the poetry faculty of the Callaloo Creative Writing Workshops.